David Le Grys aka Legro is a cyclist. He has raced at international and national level all over the world. David is also a coach and has studied NLP (Nero Linguistic Programming).

He has won 35 national elite/professional and masters championships, nine European Masters Championships, and 24 World Masters Championships.

David took a break from cycling during the early '90s while he was national sprint coach and began running to keep fit. He started with local fun runs and went on to run marathons, his best time being 2 hours 38 minutes, he eventually got back into cycling and racing again by competing in duathlons (run-bike-run).

His fastest speed on a bike was 110 mph behind Tom Walkinshaw's racing saloon car on the M42, the motorway was loaned to Dave for a day by the MOT but was unfortunately rained off before his next attempt of 135 mph.

David is now retired from racing. Many years of crashes and vigorous training has finally caught up with him, however, back surgery, open heart surgery and rheumatoid arthritis has not stopped him from riding his bike, so beit a little more leisurely.

Broken Heart is just one chapter of David's life on how he dealt with open heart surgery and the journey to recovery.

This book is dedicated to my wife, Tracy Le Grys; cardiologist and friend, Dr Nigel Stephens; cardiologist, Mr Frank Wells and ablation doctor, Tushar Salukhe.

David Le Grys

BROKEN HEART

AUSTIN MACAULEY PUBLISHERS™
LONDON • CAMBRIDGE • NEW YORK • SHARJAH

Copyright © David Le Grys 2023

The right of David Le Grys to be identified as author of this work has been asserted by the author in accordance with sections 77 and 78 of the Copyright, Designs and Patents Act 1988.

All rights reserved. No part of this publication may be reproduced, stored in a retrieval system, or transmitted in any form or by any means, electronic, mechanical, photocopying, recording, or otherwise, without the prior permission of the publishers.

Any person who commits any unauthorised act in relation to this publication may be liable to criminal prosecution and civil claims for damages.

All of the events in this memoir are true to the best of author's memory. The views expressed in this memoir are solely those of the author.

A CIP catalogue record for this title is available from the British Library.

ISBN 9781035802005 (Paperback)
ISBN 9781035802012 (ePub e-book)

www.austinmacauley.com

First Published 2023
Austin Macauley Publishers Ltd®
1 Canada Square
Canary Wharf
London
E14 5AA

David Le Grys – A Foreword

It is a great privilege to be asked to write the introduction to this compelling story.

David and I have a relationship that is unusual and perhaps unique. He is a friend, coach, teammate and patient. What success I have had as a journeyman Masters track cyclist I owe to his wise counsel and remarkable emotional intelligence as a highly respected cycling coach. I have tried to pay a little back by being his doctor.

It is tricky being a doctor to your friends. Your feelings for them intrude and you may lack the necessary sang froid that you need to make good decisions and give the right advice. You are also tempted to make short cuts and offer a glib opinion. So, when David asked my view on his troublesome cough, I held back but offered to do it properly – history, examination and special tests being the proper and time-honoured process of diagnosis.

The history offered little. The examination told the whole story. Quite unexpectedly he had obvious severe leakage of the mitral valve. The tests confirmed and gave us the details and took us on a journey which he recounts here. I was able to offer a little more help in introducing him to Mr Frank Wells – a prodigiously talented surgeon in mitral repair, which notoriously taxes surgical skills to the full. Four years later he developed atrial flutter and my signposting skills came to the fore again and allowed my colleague Tushar Salukhe to do a successful ablation.

Illness reveals our true nature. The artifice of status and class and bravado is gone and we are honestly tested. More impressive than his remarkable cycling palmares was David's acceptance of adversity, physical courage and resolve to get over it and push on. It was humbling and inspiring to be part of.

Nigel Stephens PhD FRCP Consultant Cardiologist

Open Heart Surgery? No Problem

As I write this, I am coming up to sixty years of age. Although, I am realising that my body is gradually staggering to a halt, my mind still wants to break some World-best times for track cycling in the Masters' over-sixty age group. Me being me, I not only want to put those records on the shelf, but I also want to know I am faster than the forty-year-olds which is a big deal when you are over 20 years their senior, and at the wrong end of life. A few months ago, however, when I was preparing for the 2015 World Masters Championship my body started to misbehave.

Around now, my mate Lee Povey is organising a World Record attempt for several sprinters at Aguascalientes in Mexico, on one of the fastest tracks in the world. Sprinters use this track because it is at altitude; this type of athlete does not require so much oxygen during a race, and you can cut through the thin air much quicker than at sea level. Endurance riders also train at altitude, but the benefit comes mostly only once they are back at sea level – it's all to do with haemoglobins and red blood cells which I won't go in to. With this in mind, I had arranged to stay with Lee in California at a holding camp before going with him to Mexico.

In the meantime, back in Essex, I had been training very hard and showing some good signs of being on pace for the world record over 500 metres and 200 metres, however, my recovery from my sprint efforts when training were getting worse. Whenever I made a big effort, I really struggled to get my breath – much worse than in the chapter 'death by 500's' that will be going in my second book. I told my wife, Tracy, that I was a bit concerned – the track in Aguascalientes, is nearly 2000 metres above sea level, and I would struggle even harder to recover my breath at that altitude. Tracy said I would be fine, thinking I was probably bottling it and needed a shove to get on. Privately, I was starting to think there was something seriously wrong.

A few years previously, I first met Dr Nigel Stephens at the Finchley Road team's cycling club dinner. As a practicing heart surgeon and cyclist, he arranged visits to his hospital for me to sort out an old hamstring injury I had, and in return I would coach him. Over the years, we got to know each other well and became good friends. When Dr Nigel heard about my plans in Mexico, and as he was aware of my breathing problems, he offered to examine me. Well, it wasn't quite like that. I was racing an evening track league at Lee Valley Velodrome, I won a 30 lap race and when I returned to the riders pit, I was struggling to breath and felt and looked awful according to my worried team mates. Nigel was racing that evening too and recommended I stopped racing and to come and see him.

We made arrangements for me to attend his clinic in Northwick Park Hospital, and once I arrived Dr Nigel asked me to take off my shirt so he could listen to my heart. Within 10 seconds, Dr Nigel asked how long I had this heart murmur.

I was shocked, as my doctors who had examined me many times never spotted it. An echo-cardiogram (Docs call it an 'Echo') was arranged straight away, as well as blood tests and x-rays. The doctors discovered I probably had a prolapsed mitral valve (leaky heart valve): it didn't look too bad, they said, but it needed further investigation.

I then had another Echo but this time I was on a bike. I had to ride to exhaustion while at the same time the doctors were looking at what was going on with my leaky heart valve. It was not good news. When I was getting into a state of exhaustion, the valve was letting more blood back into the heart chamber than it was pumping out: basically my lungs were filling up with blood – as my blood had to go somewhere – which would explain my breathing difficulties after a big effort.

After years of struggling to catch my breath after a sprint – after endless visits to the lung doctors, having being told it's psychological, or that I have exercise induced asthma, and that I should use my inhalers and so on – I had finally found out what was wrong with me. I was in complete shock – almost in denial – not really grasping how major this was, especially for my racing prospects, and how on earth I survived when I was in heart failure without knowing it, I will never know. While it was a relief to find this out, perhaps it could have been fatal if I continued racing? Mexico was suddenly not looking like an option.

More tests were in order to check my airways, so I had tubes down my nose going down into my bronchioles. I then had to swallow another tube to check out my swallowing issues – did I not mention my swallowing issues? As well as my breathing problems, I was also coughing and bringing up loads of phlegm. This test was to check there was not another problem going on, though the doctors suspected this was due to the leaky heart valve. I was surprised I never had a tube up my arse as all other orifices were covered.

Turning his attention back to my heart, Dr Nigel booked me in for an angiogram. I needed this to make sure that after years of smoking during my midlife crisis, my coronary arteries which supply blood to the heart, had not been narrowed or blocked. It was a weird experience all round. First I was given rohypnol and then a local anaesthetic to calm me down, I now don't really give a shit about the doctor sticking a tube into my artery in my wrist, navigating his way to inside my heart. Through this tube, Dr Nigel then injected a dye which shows up on an X-ray, which traces the blood as it travels through the heart chambers, capillaries etc, to show if there is any complications during surgery. The angiogram went fine, especially considering Dr Nigel had crashed at the track and broken his collar bone two days before running the procedure. The rohypnol was working especially well…I was in the land of the fairies. As I returned to the recovery ward, Tracy had arrived in order to drive me home. I laid down on a bed during the recovery process and then things started to go a bit wrong. What happened next was due to a combination of having not eaten, dropping sugar levels, and causing an 'episode'.

To monitor my recovery, I had a band wrapped around my wrist that was pumped up with air, and was tight enough to stop any bleeding. The nurse would gradually let off the pressure on the wrist band to slow down the bleeding and this took around an hour or so. However, in Legro-land, that didn't happen. After about two hours, the nurse returned and released a bit more air from the wrist band to check if my wound had stopped bleeding, and said, "it's going to take a bit longer." I said to Tracy, "I don't feel too good." Suddenly, I felt blood rushing to my head and my blood pressure plummeting, and I collapsed. I could hear an alarm going off in the ward, 'CARDIAC ARREST, CODE RED' and I thought to myself, *somebody is having a heart attack.* I could hear voices of lots of people around me. The alarm repeatedly bellowed 'CARDIAC ARREST, CODE RED; CARDIAC ARREST, CODE RED', and still I had not figured out that person was me. The crash crew chucked Tracy out and drew the curtains around me; the defibrillator was wheeled in and at this point, Tracy was really worried. She is a trained first responder, and knew the drill. When they started putting the pads on my chest and the stand back machine (defib) was on standby, she thought the worst.

"Can you hear me, David," someone asked. I couldn't respond but my head could, if that makes sense. My words were not coming out of my mouth, and in the commotion, Dr Nigel had been alerted and came rushing in and discovered me on the floor, all wired up ready to be resuscitated. After a quick pause, he explained that I had fainted, and that this was called in the trade as an 'episode', it happens when blood pressure drops dangerously low, and it feels very unpleasant, a lot worse than your average faint. Eventually, the curtain that surrounded me was drawn back and the defib machine was wheeled away. Gradually, all the doctors dispersed, and I was back on the bed recovering and waiting for my artery to stop bleeding. After six hours, and several attempts to release the pressure off my wrist band, I was eventually allowed to go home.

A couple of days later, while I was at home with Tracy, Dr Nigel called me to confirm what he suspected. He was happy with the angiogram results and confirmed there was no other issues going on. I had a leaky heart valve and I need an operation. I asked him if I could go to Mexico first and then have the op, Dr Nigel's response was a very big 'NO'. It suddenly dawned on me this was serious. Tracy and I didn't speak for a few minutes after the call. I think we were both in shock.

Meanwhile, Dr Nigel had contacted his colleague Dr Frank Wells, a specialist heart valve surgeon at Papworth Hospital. Within a few days, on a Wednesday, I got a call from Dr Wells while driving into Colchester with Tracy. The call was on hands free, so we both listened as he introduced himself and asked what I was doing on Saturday. He was ready to perform open heart surgery, and I accepted. To say we were gobsmacked would be an understatement.

Blimey, within a couple weeks I was going to attempt a world record, but now I faced open heart surgery! Like before, we didn't really speak a word for a few minutes. But, classic Legro, I made a joke of it to calm Tracy down.

Somehow, over the next 48 hours, I composed myself. I was almost deluded. I am normally a realist, but for some reason I still did not think this operation was a big deal. I can honestly say at that point, I was not at all worried. On the Friday afternoon, as we went to Papworth hospital – just two days after the phone call from Dr Wells – I said to Tracy, "Drop me off and pick me up in a week, no point in visiting me; it is too far to come and it is no big deal."

Legro Goes to Papworth

The drive to Papworth was surreal, it is a good 90 miles away from home. I was blanking out whether or not I would survive and was making loose chat with Tracy. At the same time, I was thinking about making plans for when I can race again. My mind was all over the place.

When we eventually arrived at Papworth, I was checked in and I had more blood tests, X-rays and an echocardiogram. I then ended up in a ward sharing with just two other patients who both had similar operations to what I was going to have. It was good to share stories and get an idea on how I might be feeling after my operation and I got on really well with the other two men who's names I have forgot, sorry. This operation means more than just a valve replacement, I am told – it will allow me to race again.

After a few hours I told Tracy to go home. "I will be fine," I said again, "the op is tomorrow about lunch time. Call the hospital, but don't come to see me, it's too far to come. I will be fine." Tracy eventually went, albeit a bit tearful, and I was left with the other two patients. We got talking about what they do and what I do.

As I was settling in, Dr Wells popped in to reassure me, and explained a little bit more about the procedure. And then, one by one, the two patients I was sharing the ward with got discharged and then I was on my own.

At this point I got a bit scared. I had no one to talk to and my mind was now totally focussed on my heart operation. I remember asking Dr Nigel questions like, does it hurt? What exactly do they do to repair a mitral heart valve? Dr Nigel explained that, basically, they split open my sternum down the centre, open up my chest so there is a large gaping hole, disconnect the heart, sever the nerves, collapse the lungs and let the life support machine take over. They then repair the valve, reconnect the heart, start it up, and the job is good and sorted. Well, he didn't say it quite like that but that's my take on it. He also said the operation will completely decondition me, whatever that meant.

After a long worrying night. I was woken up at 6 am for bloods. No breakfast, no one to talk to, Billy no mates waiting to have his heart fixed. To make things worse, the phone signal in Papworth was rubbish and I couldn't call Tracy.

Next, a very nice nurse came to see me and said she needed to shave my chest and then prepare me for the operation. She then said I had to shave my pubes. My pubes and I have been together for many years and now I was having to shave them off. The nurse did my chest and then handed me the electric razor. I looked like a teenager again.

My moment had come. I was first on the list to go to theatre that day, and a couple of porters wheeled my bed through the corridors of the hospital. It was a strange feeling, weaving through patients, doctors, nurses, gazing at the ceiling and thinking it needs a coat of paint. Very surreal. We finally arrived at theatre, and everyone was in position, checking their machines, wires, and instruments, all dressed in green, all wearing face masks. The doors closed behind me, and I was sealed in the pre-med room. I could see the doctors and nurses through the clear plastic doors.

The anaesthetist introduced himself, explained the procedure, he was cracking jokes to calm me down and said I am going to feel very relaxed shortly, and five hours later I started to come around, I was feeling very groggy.

People who have come out from under anaesthetic always have a tale to tell, but mine was a typical Legro moment. I'll set the scene: I'm in the resuscitation room, coming out of anaesthetic. My heart is fixed and reconnected and I am off the life support machine. However, I am not yet breathing on my own, and tubes were coming out of my mouth, jugular vein, arms and stomach, and there is a massive zip-like gash down the middle of my chest. By my bedside is a nurse and Tracy – Dr Wells had previously informed Tracy that the operation was a success and she could see me.

I'm semi-conscious, I can hear voices. "Come on, Dave, breathe." I hear Tracy's voice which confuses me, Why is she here? I told her not to come. "Dave you must breathe on your own, I heard from Tracy." My eyes are still shut and I am not completely aware of what is going on. "BREATH, YOU MUST DO IT ON YOUR OWN," the voices are getting louder, "breathe, Dave," – HE'S GONE, "COMEBACK, DAVE!" I hear an alarm going off, and sounds of people running towards me. I am dead, I thought. Is this what it is like to be dead? It is so peaceful; I feel like I am floating. I can still hear voices telling me to breathe. Eventually, I come round in the ward; I must have been brought back to life. The tube down my throat has gone, and my lovely wife's head is asleep on my bed. I stroke her hair and she wakes up. It was emotional for both of us; although the op was a success, there was always the thought that major heart surgery can go wrong.

As it turned out, back in the resuscitation room when I heard voices shouting 'BREATHE, DAVE!' and thought I was dead, there was actually another bloke in the room called Dave. Tracy told me this, and we sort of chuckled, but it became much funnier as the months went by. By the way, that other Dave was fine, he was OK in the end. I told Tracy to go home and get some sleep; it was late and she needs to get some proper rest, and thanked her for coming to see me.

And so it began, my long journey of recovery, and I have absolutely no idea how it is going to pan out. Papworth is one of the best heart hospitals in the world and I knew I was in good hands. I was moved to another part of the ward which only had two beds and a TV. This was great because, guess what? The Tour de France was live on ITV4 every day for next three weeks, and my bedside companion was blind and a bit deaf, so didn't mind if I had le tour on every day. Blood pressure checks, ECG, drugs, and doctors' visits were all part of the daily routine. After the first day, the pain I was in was manageable – though I could only lay on my back as it was too uncomfortable to sleep on my sides. I tried to call Tracy but the signal was still bad, and I was feeling pretty sorry for myself, to be honest. I was starting to realise what had happened and for some reason I had blanked it all out until that point.

All of a sudden, I had this horrible pain in my lower back. I knew exactly what that pain was, as I was familiar with it. Despite all the pain killers I was on, I was wriggling about in agony. I called for a nurse to inform her I have a stone in my kidney. She had a look of 'how the fuck do you know' on her face. More doctors were called and it was decided that I need a CT scan to confirm.

A wheelchair appeared and I was rushed to the CT scan from the ward. I nearly passed out getting there, the pain was unreal. When we arrived, they asked me to climb up and lay face down on what was basically a cold sheet of stainless steel. Climbing up was a big enough task in my condition, let alone lowering myself down against that cold stainless steel on my recently-opened chest. I painfully eased myself out of the wheel chair onto the platform I had to lay on. I got on my all fours and then gradually bit by bit lowered myself down on to my chest, careful of the tubes coming out of neck, arms and stomach as well as my operation wounds.

I eventually got into position, they run the scan, and it was confirmed I had a stone in the kidney. Great, that's all I need following heart surgery. I then had to get back into the wheel chair and was taken back to my ward. This whole experience completely exhausted me. Open heart surgery completely debilitates you; just standing up can leave you gasping for breath and wondering how on earth you can go from being very fit to being reduced to this state.

Back in the ward, I was given more pain killers, I was told to drink plenty and try to pee out the stone. It didn't help matters when most of my recovery in first few days was lying on my back making it even more uncomfortable for my kidney. I was on so many painkillers, and the pain did eventually subside after a couple of days, or I might have peed the stone out. Who knows, but it went as soon as it came, and was just another on a list of obstacles to my recovery.

I was lucky to have friends come and see me who would bring me treats, listen to my story, and gaze at my new zip all the way down my chest. It's great having your mates come and see you, especially when they bring jelly babies. My daily routine was now; get up, have a wash and shave, breakfast, drugs, more tests, tour de France on TV, visitors, drugs, doctors' rounds, drugs, tea, tour de France highlights, tea, more drugs, sleep. But, all I wanted all day was to see my Tracy. I was so happy when she came to see me.

After a few days it was time to take out a drain that was coming out of my stomach, two tubes that needed to come out. "It will be a bit unpleasant," the doctor said. As the doctor pulled out the first tube, there was a gurgling sound, this horrible sick feeling, and quite a lot of pain. 'A bit unpleasant' was an understatement – it was horrible. "Well done, David," he said, "now we have to do the other tube, let me know when you are ready." I suggested tomorrow perhaps, but after a few chuckles from nurses and doctor he proceeded to pull out the other tube which was as bad as the first one he removed!

With those stomach tubes gone, the line that was in my jugular vein in my neck was also removed along with the wires connected to my heart. These were just a precaution in case my heart stopped, and they would zap my heart to start again or something like that, an internal defib. I still had a line on my arm for more blood tests and drugs if needed but I could now get about a lot better. I would wander around the wards and even venture outside but I was very slow and very breathless. Just getting out of the bed was exhausting. Racing a bike again was a million miles away. Now I knew what Dr Nigel had meant by being 'deconditioned'.

I had bad days. It was not all plain sailing and because of my emotions were unstable I handled them badly. I said to Tracy on one of her visits, "I have had enough, I wish I had not had the operation," and then all of a sudden a nurse appeared. She closed the curtains, told Tracy to leave us for a moment, and told me off.

"There was a team of dedicated people including Mr Wells that worked on you, with the sole intention of making you well. The preparation for this behind the scenes takes hours and the commitment of the surgeons, and then the nurses who monitored you 24 hours a day afterwards to make sure you get better, and you want to throw it all away? You wish you hadn't had your heart operation?"

I felt ashamed. In amongst feeling sorry for myself, this nurse made me realise how lucky I am, and to get a grip. Tracy was allowed back in and the tears in her eyes said it all. I am a rubbish patient; I really had to man up. The more you feel sorry for yourself, the more you feel the pain; the more you feel like you want to give in, the more you really do have to rise above it and start to think positively no matter what happens. I was full of remorse and apologised to the nurse and Tracy: I needed that telling off, I really did. Just for the record, I was told of the changes which would affect me in my recovery period. The physiological change for me would be massive, my body and brain did not understand the shift from a high level of fitness to being totally deconditioned.

Let me give you an idea what deconditioned is like. When just standing up makes you breathless and panting, a slow walk around the room is so hard you have to sit down to recover after a minute or two. Climbing stairs one step at a time leaves you hanging on to the rail, breathing very heavily, and having to recover before the next step. When you finally get to the top of the stairs, you are so out of breath, and completely exhausted it would take a good 10 minutes to get over it. Your emotions go all over the place; I still get very upset over the smallest of things – that's not funny when you're watching EastEnders and you burst out crying half way through. It has something to do with a nerve that was severed during surgery, causing all sorts of malfunctions, emotions, mindset, forgetfulness. When you think about it, my brain was kept alive by the life support machine, my brain had no heart beat for 5 hours and then my brain had a heartbeat, no wonder it got confused!

As I gradually got stronger, after a few of days, the line in my arm was removed and I was walking further and further. Outside my ward was a lake, and I would go outside and have a walk around it. I could stop and look at the fish and sit down on the benches scattered around the footpath to recover. I was lucky it was summer time, nice and warm. It gave me time to ponder and I further realised how lucky I am. If I had not had coached Dr Nigel I would not be walking around this lake on a summer's day. I still struggled not to get breathless, I was still not used to being so unfit and out of condition.

I continued to walk around that lake, lap after lap, resting and then going again. I started timing myself and ended up practically running around but I couldn't do it for long. Tracy diligently came to see me each day; so much for the 'just drop me off and I'll see you in a week'. I so looked forward to seeing her and my mates that took the trouble to come and see me, but I knew I wasn't a pretty sight with my new zip-up chest.

After a few days, I was into a new routine; breakfast, a walk around the wards, the doctor's visits, another walk around the wards, venturing outside for a few laps of the lake, then a bit of Le Tour. During this I would be having blood pressure checks, lunch, and the occasional cardio-echo test. By this time I was quite tired and often slept through some of le Tour, or I would get a visitor that would wake me up. Sleeping and feeling exhausted was something I was trying to get over. There is another level of tiredness which I had never experienced.

One day while I was walking around the lake and I stumbled across this bloke on a bench looking a lot like Doddsy. "Doddsy," I said, "what you doing here?" He came to see me out of the blue, he even brought diet coke and chocolate which I wasn't really allowed but consumed while hiding behind a bush, watching the ducks. We went back to my room to watch le Tour and then another mate Lee Rowe turned up. It was great having mates that care along with my family and other friends that came to see me, thank you to them all. When we all went out for a walk around the lake, I think Doddsy and Lee realised I was going to take a long time to get over this – they were barely walking and I was struggling to keep up.

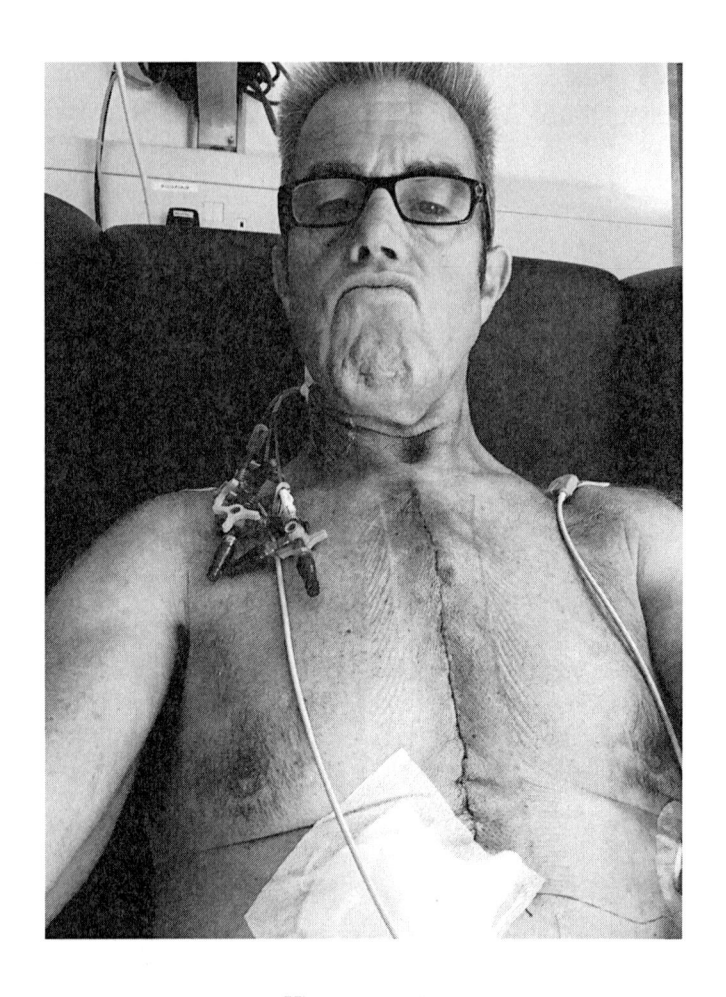

Heart operation

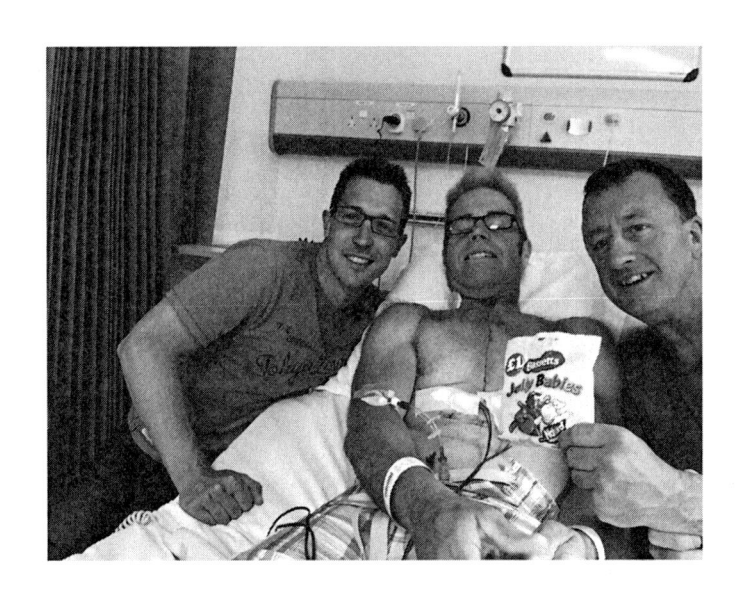

Post operation with friends

Legro interviewing Dr Nigel

Legro And Dr Nigel

Legro and wife Tracy in Majorca

Racing

World masters champion

Legro Coming Home
Tears of a Clown

The day came when I was to be discharged, but my physio told me that I had to show I could walk up a flight of stairs. What she didn't know was, I had been practicing this for past two days. It is probably the hardest exercise I have ever done in my life – walking upstairs, stopping every step to get my breath back, It took a while to climb them but I made it to the top and the physio signed me off.

Waiting to be released could take an hour, or it could be all day – it is dependent on how busy everyone one is – plus there were all my notes for my GP and my drugs to sort out. I was on three painkillers a day plus some liquid morphine for when it got really bad. The pain was mainly in my sternum which the kind Dr Wells split open to get at my heart. He told me he had wired it up twice because he knew I was going to get back to racing and would be "giving it some".

Tracy turned up to bring me home, and after saying my farewells to fellow patients. I had made friends within different parts of the ward – all of whom were in for heart operations ranging from transplants to bypasses. We all had something in common; a full chest zip and another chance in life, which can bring complete strangers together like old friends. When we wished each other all the best, we meant it. It was a bit emotional, and the same goes to those brilliant doctors and nurses. I am not knocking other hospitals, but Papworth is in a league above the rest.

Getting out of Papworth is not easy, having to go down stairs and walk to carpark with poor Tracy having to carry everything. When it came to getting in the car, I couldn't do it. Putting my leg in, leaning across and grabbing the door was stretching my stiches, and I was feeling faint doing this. I eventually got in. It was scary because I thought I was going to fall – Dave Le Grys, the man that has had so many high-speed bike crashes, was scared to fall over getting into a car!

The journey home was interesting to say the least. I was clutching my chest and at every bump I would scream out, even though Tracy was trying her hardest to miss them. When we got home, I was feeling quite frail, and getting out of the car was equally as hard as getting in. It was nice to be home but the journey knocked the stuffing out of me. I felt so vulnerable, so helpless and so weak. What if I got attacked? How could I defend myself, or how could I protect Tracy? Apparently, this is a normal reaction following heart surgery.

So apart from feeling unsecure, vulnerable, weak, tired, breathless, emotional and in pain, everything was all good. I am not feeling sorry for myself here, I just want to explain how I actually felt. To top it all, I could see things. Like bubbles and strange shapes, which got me confused. Nevertheless, it was great being home. I knew I had a long haul in front of me getting back to fitness, and it wasn't going to be easy, but I didn't quite realise how much the next few weeks were not going to be good.

Tracy had a lot of time off work because of me, and now I was home, she needed to get back to work. She was concerned about leaving me home alone, but I assured her I would be OK, because we had the gardener around to keep an eye on me. She had pre-made my lunch and tea so I didn't need to carry it or do anything that I couldn't manage. In any case, I could call her at work if I had to. I was told at Papworth I need regular exercise and rest, so Tracy thought I would get up and walk around the living room a few times then sit down. However, Legro's idea of exercise was a two mile walk around a field.

As soon as she went to work, I was off walking around the field, stopping every five paces to get my breath back. Boy, was I out of condition! At least it was summer time and the weather was good. It took me over an hour to walk around that field, after many stops and me whinging, crying my eyes out practically all the way round – not because I was in pain, but because I was so emotional and out of condition.

Tracy would call me from time to time in her breaks to check on me, making sure I took my drugs and had my lunch. Before I tell you what I did next, I must explain I was on a big downer. I felt unwell, tired, and insecure. I was depressed, but I don't know why. My heart has been fixed, but I guess the recovery was harder than I expected, and I was slowly losing that Legro fighting spirit. So, I instinctively switched to my other coping strategy; my sense of humour.

Those of you that know me and follow me on Facebook would know I did video updates of my rehab and recovery. It was the start of many video updates that led to Tracy getting very upset. My first video was done just a few days after I was back home. Tracy was at work and Mollie my stepdaughter had been staying with us with her boyfriend, Jamie. While Mollie and Jamie were still asleep, I sneaked out with a plastic bag containing, snorkel, flippers and googles. During my morning walk, I stopped about half way around the field and got changed into a pair of swimming trunks, and then I put on the snorkel and flippers.

This was to be my first video of me walking across the fields, showing just the views of my walk and me trying to talk and breathing heavy. At this point, I was not in camera shot.

As I panned the camera across the countryside towards myself, it revealed me in my snorkelling gear (and a great shot of my chest scar), explaining I that feel pretty good and am making good progress. That was exactly what I wanted my viewers to see and her.

After filming the video I got changed back in to my clothes, and finished my morning walk, and to be honest this was harder than the last time. When I finally got back home, Mollie was up cooking breakfast and was unaware of my morning's activities. I settled down on the sofa and was recovering from my walk. Looking back it was crazy, and I wasn't feeling that good.

After an hour or so, I made a phone call to my mate, Dave Marsh (Marshy) and, as we were chatting, I started to feel a bit faint. All of a sudden, I dropped the phone on the floor and said to Mollie, "I don't feel too good," and at that point, I fainted – and it was a bad faint. I thought I was going to die.
https://www.youtube.com/watch?v=IpqjSfnnrl4&feature=youtube

While I was breathing heavily and felt virtually lifeless, Mollie said, "Are you shitting me?" I could not even respond. All I can remember is Mollie calling 999 and the paramedics arriving. I was given oxygen, and had another ECG, all the stats suggested I was OK, but I needed to go back to hospital to make sure.

Mollie called my sister, Jenny, and Tracy to let them know what had happened. Tracy met me at Colchester hospital together with Jenny. Jenny said I was doing a Hollywood, Tracy was worried sick and in the brief moments in between the doctors taking blood from my artery and various other tests, Tracy was by my side. I said I felt like something was wrong. I was wired up to a defib machine in case I was going to have a heart attack. When the doctors finally came back with the results, Tracy and Jenny were with me around the bed as I was told I had post-op pneumonia.

The doctor said maybe I was over doing it, and when I showed him my video, he could not believe his eyes. I was told off with tongue in cheek as he informed me of the risks I was taking, while at the same time commending me for making his day. I spent the next three days in hospital being monitored and more tablets to take along with my other drugs – this time antibiotics were added to the list. I am not knocking Colchester hospital but here was a few times my breathing was not good and I was in distress, and the night shift nurses just walked past me like there was nothing wrong. That would not have happened at Papworth – the nurses there were more switched on. Anyway, Tracy would visit me when she could, I got more and more bored and started to hate the nurses at Colchester. To be fair, some of them were really good – but most were from agencies, and seemed not to give a shit. I saw one of these nurses have a go at a patient next to me who must have had dementia. He was made to look a fool as he was taunted and ignored. I gave that nurse a piece of my mind, but I should have reported him.

I couldn't wait to get out of there and was pleased when I did. They needed the beds, and once I was well enough to get better at home, I was stuck in my prison home again. Tracy was too scared to go to work, as she could not trust me and was worried I might do something stupid and collapse.

As the days dragged by, I was not showing much signs of improvement. I was still breathless and my chest still hurts, but I still did my walks and rested in between. I knew this was going to take a long time, which isn't easy though for someone as impatient as me. But from then on, I rested when I should have been resting.

About a week later at home, while Tracy was at work, I had another episode, I had passed out. When I came too, I called 999, my heart was pounding and I got a bit scared, within 20 minutes the paramedics arrived and performed the normal tests. It was decided I needed to go to hospital again as a precaution. Oh dear!

Tracy was informed, and again she met me at Colchester hospital, tears rolling down her cheeks. "I can't take any more of this," she told me. I felt terrible. I wanted to get better – I was resting and doing everything I was told to do and it still all seemed to go wrong. More tests; ECGs and blood tests, including another painful artery blood test – I really don't like those ones. Fortunately, I was discharged a few hours later. It was just a faint, but the blood pressure did drop to a dangerous low. It's all part of getting over heart surgery I guess.

Papworth Hospital would call me every now and again to see how I was doing. They also gave us an emergency number to contact if I was unwell or worried. I did call a couple of times when I was experiencing irregular heartbeats or breathing issues. They would explain what was happening and this put my mind to rest, as some of the symptoms are quite frightening.

Meanwhile back at the ranch, I was at an all-time low, I was thinking about doing another video update. My friend and neighbour, Steve Clark, lent me some fancy-dress costumes including a Bin Laden mask, clown outfit, and various wigs and props. My crazy mind went into overtime, dreaming up funny videos which allowed me to give updates on my recovery.

Week three after my op, I was still feeling quite unwell so, I booked to see my local GP. Tracy went with me, but dropped me off while she went to find a park for the car. I ended up with an appointment with one of the doctors that originally diagnosed me with exercise-induced asthma. His surgery was on the second floor, and when I was buzzed to see him, I knocked and entered his room, nearly collapsing from exhaustion, after climbing the stairs. I knocked on his door, and he said, "come in."

As I sat down trying to get my breath, he said to me, "And what can we do for you?" I slowly lifted my head, I said, "If you bothered to look at your computer screen, you will see why I am here." As the doctor started to read my notes off his screen, I could hear his voice buckle. "I see you have had heart surgery." He continued to read, and suddenly became very supportive and helpful. I reminded him of when I saw him about four years previously, and several times since, about my breathing problems and despite all the examinations I was convinced I needed an inhaler, or that it was all in my head. He back-pedalled, and was fumbling though some old files justifying his findings, but I was in no mood to defend myself or take it further as I was feeling quite rough.

He did a quick examination and then rang Colchester hospital, saying I need to get checked over urgently. Tracy had arrived after parking the car and was horrified to find I was to be re-admitted back to hospital. Off we went, again wondering what to expect. What we were about to experience was devastating.

I had the usual checks, heart, ECG bloods etc and then had to see a doctor, after some chin rubbing, humming and ahhhing, I asked him what his thoughts were. He said there is possible heart failure, or the heart valve could be infected, and so he sent me off for an x-ray.

As Tracy and I went off to get x-rayed, I said, "Oh well, that's the end of Legro." Tracy burst out crying, causing me to do the same and we were both in shock. Even after all I had been through, my future doesn't look bright. I had the x-ray and had to wait four hours before we could see the doctor to review the findings; four hours of anxious pacing, wondering what the hell is going to happen.

When we eventually got called to see the doctor, another doctor was also present, he was more of a heart specialist and had worked with the Tinko Saxo Professional cycling team. He said I could have an infection in the heart valve, and I need to take it easy – pack up cycling and rest. I looked at Tracy in disbelief. I am bloody well not going to stop cycling after Dr Wells had fixed me.

When we got home, Dr Wells called me, as Colchester hospital had informed him of all my visits. He summoned me back to Papworth for a further two days of thorough testing. When I saw Dr Wells, he said it is very unlikely I have a valve infection and that all my symptoms are consistent with heart surgery recovery. After many tests including ECG, Echo and Obs (observations) I was informed that I was OK and was allowed home. Dr Wells was not happy with Colchester hospital for causing me grief as well as giving me bad advice, and assured me I will be able to return to cycling and, in time, I could race again.

Back home, but this time feeling more positive. Although, Tracy and I were still suffering the shock of going from heart failure to be given a clean bill of health. Back to normal life again, and back to my routine. Every day I would go for a walk, and it was a pleasure to be alive and to be living out in the country an enjoying the views. I increased my walks to an hour a day, sometimes twice a day, and I continued my video updates every week, which if you remember, had begun when I first walked out in the field half naked in snorkel and flippers.

What can I say? If you have seen the updates, you would have concluded one of three things; that I was really losing it, that I was attention seeking, or that I was just finding ways to cope with the fallout from my surgery. All my life, all I ever wanted to do was to make people smile, I like people to enjoy life; if I can make them happy, even at my cost, I'm happy. So these videos might sound and look crazy but it was my way of overcoming my depression and making people laugh at my expense.

While I was uploading these crazy videos, my poor suffering wife was getting more and more upset with me. I would see her face when she looked on Facebook, and saw all the kind words and the comments about how well I am doing. "Why are you doing this? You are a long way from being back to normal, nobody sees you when you are having a bad day, they only see you when you are doing those silly videos." I tried to explain to Tracy, it really was the only way I know to combat this and move on. I think she understood but was hurting inside knowing I wasn't actually feeling nowhere near as good as my videos suggested.

Legro back on his bike

By now, I had been doing a lot of walking, and started to think about riding my bike after week four. Eventually, I plucked up the courage and ventured out on my road bike. It was a nerve-wracking experience just getting on my bike, but it was too painful on my chest and sternum, so I tried my mountain bike – the upright position made it easier and pain free. Nobody knew when I slipped out for a ride; I would go out for 10 minutes at first, then 30, then an hour. It was great to get out on my bike and feel the wind in my face.

One of the hills I live by was very challenging. Normally, I would just ride up and not even get out of breath, but right now I would go up so slow and was breathing out of my arse. At the top of the hill it would take me 10 minutes just to breathe normally again after stopping at the top.

After six weeks, I went to see Dr Nigel. He checked me over and said, I should have been a case study. My recovery was probably six months ahead of a normal 60-year-old, despite my setbacks, and all the tests came out good. We talked about perhaps going out for short bike rides. I confessed I had already tried it but never mentioned I was doing an hour to 90 minutes a day.

I started to go out with Tracy on our mountain bikes, but I struggled to ride with her even though she was riding easy around 10 mph. She would drop me on all the hills I just could not keep up with her – she wasn't even trying to drop me either. It was a horrible experience being this unfit but it was great to be alive and riding with my wife.

Over time, I began to hang on to Tracy on the hills. The fitness was coming and I was feeling more positive, but I knew it was a long way to full fitness.

Over the coming weeks, I would gradually extend my rides. That hill I was struggling to get up was getting better, and then I started to think about getting back on the track. Finally, I booked a session at Lea Valley Olympic Velodrome.

It was great to be back on the track and riding with my mates again. I managed to keep up with most of the training although I would get dropped towards the end of the warm up, breathing very heavily. I went the following week and even in the space of those seven days, I was keeping up and riding more comfortably. By nine weeks post-op, I was back on the track. I continued to ride on the road, trying to ride most days, building on my base. I would also start to include a few digs to test my fitness. It was coming, but I could only hold a hard effort for a few seconds. Even at this point, I was overwhelmed at how unfit I felt.

I am a very driven person. This can be a good thing, as I am full of positive thoughts, always aiming for a goal – nothing will stop me. It can also be a bad thing, particularly when I overdo it. Finding a balance between building fitness and trying to push myself was tricky. I was governed by a brain that was programmed to train as an elite athlete, while having the body of an asthmatic ant carrying heavy shopping.

In weeks 10, 11 and 12, I was able to train harder. I limited my hardest efforts to mainly training on the rollers. I would do one-minute sprints, trying to hold a cadence of 170rpm (revs per minute) for the whole of the 60 seconds. However, after only 20 seconds at this cadence, I was already starting to blow – holding the cadence for another 40 seconds caused me to start panicking, struggling to catch a breath. I would then give myself four minutes to recover and go again. The same with the two-minute efforts, with a cadence of around 140-150rpm. That was even more unpleasant.

The other days I would ride steady on the road, and venture into the gym once or twice a week. If I did overdo it, I would rest or do an easy recovery ride. My plan was to be able to race after at 18 weeks post-op. Dr Nigel and I had decided it was doable. I need to train smart.

Legro's First Race Post-Op

By 18 weeks, I was racing in the Tuesday night track league. I was actually racing – can you believe that? I had gone from walking a few paces and exhausting myself, to racing my bike in under five months. On the day of the race, I was shitting myself from the moment I woke up, waiting to begin loading up my car and driving to London. I put a lot of pressure on myself, feeling like I needed to win, but in reality I only needed to go there, get round, and finish each race. Job done.

When I arrived, I went straight to the canteen and had a large coffee and a couple of expresso shots. Doddsy was there to help me that evening, along with other riders that had also turned up early to avoid the rush hour. As we drank the coffee, I was getting more nervous. It felt like my first race ever and I was pretending to be so calm and cool. During warm up on my rollers, however, I didn't feel too bad. Doddsy asked how I was, and I said I was good, and that I was not going to do anything stupid. The time came to line up for our first race, a 30-lap scratch race.

It was a shock to the system. I was under geared but I can pedal fast so I was OK, but boy it was fast for a category B race – we averaged 29mph. I was hanging on for grim death on some laps but managed to hang on, I didn't ride to win, I just wanted to finish. I was once again breathing out my arse when we eventually got the bell for the final lap, and I was placed about 7th or 8th and going flat out. However, something happened in my mind, that when I heard the bell, I started to sprint, I didn't think I had it in me and I was too far back to do anything, but on the back straight I was overtaking riders, and going into turn 3 and 4, I was flying over the top and ended up 3rd.

It was close, and to be honest I could have won it if I was positioned nearer the front. I don't want to sound like one of those riders that come up with excuses, but I wasn't positioned well because at that point I had no intention of going for the win. After the race, so many nice people came up and congratulated me. One rider said, "If you are beating me now, you are going to crucify me when you get fitter."

Doddsy told me off for sprinting at the end of the race but also said well done. I warmed down on the rollers and that race left me completely exhausted. I felt like I had turned myself inside out. I rode the rest of the races just hanging on – I had nothing left in the tank, but I managed to finish all the races which was my original intention.

Driving home I was a bit emotional. I called Tracy to let her know I was coming home and told her how I went. I was nowhere near the fitness I wanted to be, but I was rather pleased with what I had managed. From open heart surgery to racing, Legro is back. However, that first race turned out to be a fluke. The following track league races, I was struggling and back to breathing out of my arse.

I had to take stock. All muscle memory, power, strength and fitness had been wiped. I had to remember only a short time ago I could hardly climb the stairs. It was only the bastard in me that got me to race after only 18 weeks.

I still have a long way to go. I might not even get close to where I want to be but it won't be for the want of trying. My aim at the time of writing was to ride the 2016 National Masters Track Championships and hopefully the World Masters Track Championships.

Post comment since writing the manuscript Dave Le Grys won the National Masters 500m TT and then went to Los Angeles USA to ride the World Masters Track Championships. He won Bronze in the sprint and Bronze in the Team sprint along with Adrian Dent and Mark Wiffen.

Dave's Wife Tracy's Version of Events

Dave's trip to Mexico was fast approaching when he went to see Dr Nigel. When he was sent for further tests, I thought that everything would be alright and that they were just playing it safe because of the level Dave competes at.

I even said to Dave that everything would be fine, "don't worry and get yourself ready to break some world records." Dave would often come home from a hard training session complaining of not able to get his breath and was always tired, I kept saying it will be fine.

I remember saying that, whatever the hospital said, he should get on the flight and things could be all sorted out when he returned.

That was until the phone call came on the Friday night, 26th June. Dave put the call onto speakerphone and we both listened quietly to what Dr Nigel was saying. Dave had a faulty heart valve and it needed repairing. He began explaining what was going on, and then Dave asked the question that was on both of our minds – could he go to Mexico?

There was a pause on the other end of the line, and then the answer came which we didn't expect. No, the valve needed to be replaced or repaired soon, and if Dave went to Mexico in his condition there was a chance that he might not come back alive. When we put the phone down it didn't seem real – to be honest, even now months have passed since the operation, it still feels like the phone call was about someone else.

We agreed that we needed to go and talk to Dave's mum, sister and brother-in-law, who don't live far away from us. We went around, told them the news, and as we left, we called my mum on the car phone and tell her too.

We were all in total shock – how could a man that was sprint training every day on his bike at 40mph, who was ready to go and break two world records, be ill enough to need an operation straight away? They must be wrong.

I remember thinking that the hospital must have got it wrong, and that we would get another call soon telling us it was a mistake. But that call never came.

On Wednesday 1st July, Dave was driving me to work when his phone rang. It was Mr Frank Wells who we were due to see on the Thursday to discuss the operation. He asked if Dave was free on the Saturday. Both of us said 'yes' without asking why, and he replied, "That's good, I've got a free slot Saturday morning and can do the operation then." Suddenly this was getting real!

The appointment went past in a blur, we sat and listened to what was going to happen and went home to pack a bag for his hospital stay.

Dave told me to drop him off on the Friday and not go back to see him until the hospital discharged him and I could collect him. I should have got that in writing because that never happened, but thinking about it after all this time makes me smile – to think it would be that simple!

On the Friday I took Dave up to Papworth Hospital and stayed with him for a couple of hours while he had bloods taken, settled in, and made friends with the men in the ward. I left and went home knowing that I wouldn't see him again until after the operation. I wanted to keep things as normal as possible and went out on my bike when I got home – little did I know that normal wasn't going to be an option for the next few weeks.

After I left the hospital, the two men on the ward had been discharged and Dave had been sitting alone thinking about the things that were going to happen. At one point he didn't want the operation anymore, and wanted to come home. I didn't collect him. We spoke on the Friday night and Saturday morning right up until they took him down to the operating theatre at 12.

I didn't sleep much on the Friday night and tried to have a normal morning, doing the house work and the like. The poor fridge took the brunt of it, and was cleaned and bleached inside and out, a job that always gets put off until you need to keep occupied. My mum had told me the best thing to do was keep busy and I did – I went shopping, did all the cleaning and went out on my bike all before 2pm. Only two more hours to use up before Dave came out of surgery, so I sat down, put the TV on and watched. This was not the best choice I have ever made, as I spent those hours crying over other people's lives.

Mr Wells called at 4.30 pm to say that the operation had gone really well, and that Dave was going to go to the critical care unit to be looked after and would be there overnight. I asked if it was alright to visit and was told that I could go up to the hospital anytime. I got ready and left the house not knowing at that stage what I could expect when I got there. On the way to the hospital, I called my mum to let her know that Dave had come through the operation and she explained to me in great detail what machines he would be hooked up to, what he would look like and exactly what I could expect to see and feel when I got to Papworth.

My dad had been in and out of hospital a lot before he died. He had a kidney transplant and cancer, and my mum's experiences gained throughout this terrible time really helped me. She was always one step ahead of the situation, telling me what to expect, and how I would feel, being my shoulder to lean on. I am eternally grateful to her for her support.

I got to the hospital to find Dave attached to numerous machines, one sedating him, one breathing for him, and drainage tubes spilled out of him. After all the advice my mum had given me on the journey up, I wasn't fazed at the sight but I still burst into tears. I think that was because I knew at that moment that I was going to have to be that strong one for a while, and anyone that knows Dave well would be able to imagine how that would be no easy feat by any means. He doesn't do ill at all!

I didn't leave the hospital that night until about midnight. I waited until Dave had come around fully from all of the aesthetic, knew what was going on, and that I had been there. I got home to my mum calling the home phone and my daughter calling my mobile, both checking that I had got home safely. I thought I would sleep like a log, but no such luck. I received text and Facebook messages all night asking about Dave, and I called the hospital myself at 6 am to see how he was. I spoke to my mum around 9 am and told her how tired I was, and she told me turn off the mobile and sleep. I obeyed, but how guilty did I feel when on waking I found missed calls from the hospital! I called them back straight away and found out that they were calling to tell me first that Dave had been moved back to a ward and second that Dave wanted to know when I was visiting. So much for drop me off and pick me up in a week!

I went up to Papworth to see him and found him sat up in bed. He didn't look too bad for a man that had a serious operation, though he did feel incredibly sorry for himself. Dave doesn't like being ill, and he is a terrible patient – lying in bed is something that he doesn't ever do. I had been worried about the scar from the operation, as I knew that it would look like a zip down the front of his chest. I couldn't look at it. In critical care it had been covered up so it hadn't bothered me, but now it was out there for all to see, getting fresh air to help it heal. Luckily, the Tour de France was on so I managed to watch the television for most of my visit, and spent the rest of it looking at Dave's face.

While visiting on the Wednesday, Dave's friend, Neil Campbell, came up as well. On the way home we stopped for a meal, and one of the questions he asked was 'how do you cope with the scar?' I had to own up that I hadn't looked at it, and to be honest I still haven't.

Dave was in hospital for a week and I visited him every day whilst still doing my day job. This was really draining on me but I always tried not to let him know how hard it was. I hadn't had the major operation, had I? But on one particular occasion Dave was feeling really down in the dumps and was in a lot of pain. He had a kidney stone on top of everything else, and the hospital had called me out of work to go and see him. I got there to find him quite poorly and fed up. I sat there talking to him and he said to me that he wished he hadn't had the operation at all, and should have taken a chance on things the way that they were. A nurse at the next bed to us had heard what Dave had said, looked at me, and saw that I was just about to burst into tears. She then politely told me to leave the ward, and I got up and left. Dave apparently got a rather lengthy lecture from the nurse and never said anything like that again. Though I doubt that any of us in his situation would feel any different.

In just two weeks, Dave had gone from being a really healthy person, training for two world record attempts in Mexico, to a man that was laid out in bed recovering from surgery, wondering if he ever be able to ride his bike to the same level again.

I collected Dave from the hospital on the Friday after his operation and took him home. This was one of the hardest drives I had ever done, as I had to try and avoid every pothole, bump in the road, and any hard breaking as the seat belt cut into his chest. If I thought we were over the hardest part of this experience I was wrong, very wrong.

Dave and I got through that first night and I went off to work knowing that the family were going to check on him throughout the day, so I didn't have to worry about him. I had been at work an hour when I got a call from Dave to say that he felt terrible and had called an ambulance. I called back to see what was going on about 30 minutes later, and on finding out Dave was going to the hospital, I left work. I got to the hospital to find Dave's sister there already.

Dave was being assessed in the resus department, and we were shown into a relative's room. I remember Jenny saying that Dave always wanted to be centre of attention and that there was probably nothing wrong with him. It turned out that Dave had pneumonia and needed more medication. Apparently, this is common after a heart operation, but why did nobody tell us?

Dave spent that night in Colchester hospital.

The next week was a rollercoaster of doctor's visits and sleepless nights. No position was comfortable for him to sleep in, he had palpitations, felt ill if he didn't eat and felt worse if he ate too much. I felt like everything was against us at that point.

Baths were something of a mission, and as we don't have a shower, there was no way around it. Dave would get into the bath okay but getting out was tiring for both of us. He had to swivel himself around so he was on his knees and I would then have to gently help him up – sounds simple, but it was far from it! Dave would often feel weak and got tired so quickly that the effort it took for him to stand up would often take it out of him and if I tried to help, I would inevitably hurt him. If I tried to stand him up by putting my arms under his armpits, not only did I hurt his chest but I ended up soaking wet. If I tried to pull him up, that hurt his arms and pulled at his stiches. In the end I had to leave him to it and he eventually found a way to get out on his own, which left him tired and grumpy.

Things did settle down over the next couple of weeks, but we did have to go back to Colchester hospital a few times when the pain got too bad or if Dave couldn't breathe properly. All of this became normal. He got his sense of humour back and started to put videos of his progress on Facebook, all of which were funny and aimed at amusing his friends, but for me it was tearing me apart, Dave was still very ill and he is telling the world he is fine, I found that hard to deal with to be honest.

My daughter, Mollie, and her boyfriend came home at the end of July to spend a few days with us. Dave was doing well by then, and we all had a good time. I went to work on the Sunday and thought that all would be well – how wrong could I be?

Dave went off out and did one of his videos, which involved walking through a field in flippers, mask and snorkel. You really have to see these videos to believe them! When he got back he was talking to a friend on the telephone and suddenly started to feel terrible, unable to breathe properly and fell to the floor. His friend was still on the phone and could hear all that was going on, and so could Mollie from the kitchen. When she walked into the lounge, she said to Dave, "Are you shitting me?" Something that she says she will always feel guilty for. Mollie and her boyfriend called the ambulance and stayed with Dave until they took him to hospital. They already had plans and people to meet, so couldn't go to the hospital with him. Dave said he would be fine and that they should go.

I went on lunch at work and found texts and missed calls from both Dave and Mollie on my mobile phone. I called Dave who told me what had happened, and that he was at the hospital waiting to be seen. I said I would come up but he insisted that he was alright. I decided to call the hospital myself and the nurse that I spoke to said that I really should go up there so I did. When I got there a doctor was just going to talk to Dave and told us that they thought that he had a minor heart attack – is there such a thing? They scanned him and did x-rays of his chest to see what was going on, and decided that they wanted to keep him in overnight. So yet again I went home, packed him a bag – by now we were both pros at this.

They kept Dave on a monitor overnight and decided that he could go home on the Monday as they could find nothing wrong. Neil picked him up for me in his lunch break as I was at work and things seemed to settle down a little bit. Dave still felt unwell and I did my normal thing and said, "If you feel bad enough, you should go to see the doctor again." To my surprise, he did!

We went to the surgery and the doctor's room was upstairs – by the time Dave got up to his room he was out of breath and felt terrible. We sat down and he looked at Dave and asked what was wrong? Dave very politely said, "Well if you had read my notes you would know."

What I didn't know was that Dave and the doctor had history – this was the doctor that for years had been telling Dave that he had exercise induced asthma and had been sending him home with different inhalers. He hadn't picked up on the fact that it was actually a leaky heart valve.

The doctor quietly sat there and read the notes, and then he started to print off paperwork. When it had all printed, he handed it to Dave. Years ago, he had sent Dave to have a check on his heart and those were the results – it felt like he was covering his own back even though a test result from about six years ago hardly seemed relevant now!

He sent us straight up to the hospital so that they could assess Dave and check him over. After all that we had been through I didn't think there wasn't anything that could surprise us but oh how wrong I was.

The doctors checked Dave over and sent him for a chest x-ray. They then told us that they thought that there could be an infection in the repaired heart valve, or that Dave had heart failure. They said that this was probably the time for him to start thinking about giving up cycling, racing and training.

They then sent us back to the waiting room and left us there for four hours, Dave said, "Well that's the end of Legro then," and I sat there in tears. Just when you thought things could not get any worse, life surprises you and not in a good way.

The doctor called us back into the treatment room and introduced us to a heart specialist. He talked to us about what he thought was happening, and said that he wanted to have an echo cardiogram done. He also reiterated that he thought an infection in the heart valve or heart failure were possibilities.

Then he dropped the bombshell. Dave asked if he would be able to get back on his bike and the specialist said that he didn't think so, and that perhaps it was time that Dave was thankful for what he had achieved in the past and to gracefully give up both racing and training. He also said that he knew what cyclists put their bodies through, as he had worked with the Tinkoff-Saxo team – that was what he was basing his advice on. He then shook both of our hands and left the room. I burst into tears and at that moment, a nurse poked her head in the door. She saw that we were both upset, said she would be back in a few minutes and left. When she returned, she brought the heart specialist back with her. He asked if we were alright and I said no – we had gone through so much in the last three weeks and we were still taking it all in – it felt like we weren't in control anymore. He said that we should concentrate on one thing, and that was that Dave was still alive and that we had had a lucky break, had Doctor Nigel not have examined him, it would have been a different story.

We went home in a bit of a state to say the least. However, Dave then spoke to Papworth hospital and they were very surprised at what the doctors at Colchester had said. They decided that he needed to go in for a couple of days and have a host of tests done so that they could evaluate what exactly was going on with Dave's body.

They did this within a few days and said that there was nothing wrong, no infection or anything – it was just the healing process and because Dave had been so fit before the operation, his body was in shock at everything that it had been through and was just playing up.

Things after that started to settle down once more. Whilst I was at work, he started to go out on his mountain bike without me knowing, when I saw one of his video's showing him crashing on a mountain bike, it wasn't real by the way, just Dave's way of having more fun and pretending he is fine (rolls eyes) so we started riding out together. This was great for me, as when we usually go out Dave's easy ride often sees me lagging behind, but I was dropping him now. Once I even had to leave him sat in a bus shelter while I finished my ride and went back for him – I felt like I'd won the lottery! As he got better, he started to go out on his own with me knowing. It didn't mean that I didn't stop worrying about him every time that he left the house, but it did get easier with time.

Imagine my horror when he said that his first race on the track was going to be in early December, 18 weeks after surgery. I was not happy at all. What if he fell off or was brought off? I never went to watch or help him at the track while he was training because my nerves wouldn't have coped with it. Being wrapped in bubble wrap, as I would have liked him to be, was not a look he wanted…

Was there any stopping this man? To be honest, I don't think there was, or ever will be, anything that can.

The Final Chapter

You will probably think I am nuts, and I would agree with you. I am hoping apart from telling my story, it could help others that are going to have open heart surgery, that you are in very good hands.

My story has a mixture of fear, emotional empathy, denial, plain stupidity and partly soul destroying, however, the outcome is uplifting and hopefully give you hope.

I did have an ablation, a year or so, after heart surgery as I had a little set back, I now am fully recovered and have regular yearly checks with Dr Nigel.

I eventually had to stop racing my bike as I had other issues with my spine, and that's another story, however, I can ride my bike albeit not that fast any more. I have slowed down a lot and now enjoy the stuff I never did much while I was racing, spending more time with my wife, walking, going away on holiday and living the dream with our grandchildren.

To my readers, the reason for this book is to try and understand my behaviour before, during and after heart surgery. So, I started to write a diary and then became part of a book I am writing, an autobiography of my life and this is just one chapter.